MW01452789

Greetings from STUART FLORIDA

Greetings from STUART FLORIDA

Greetings from STUART FLORIDA

Greetings from STUART FLORIDA

Greetings from STUART FLORIDA

Greetings from STUART FLORIDA

Greetings from STUART FLORIDA

Greetings from STUART FLORIDA

Greetings from STUART FLORIDA

Greetings from STUART FLORIDA

Greetings from STUART FLORIDA

Greetings from STUART FLORIDA

Greetings from STUART FLORIDA

Greetings from STUART FLORIDA

Greetings from STUART FLORIDA

Greetings from STUART FLORIDA

Greetings from STUART FLORIDA

Greetings from STUART FLORIDA

Greetings from STUART FLORIDA

Greetings from STUART FLORIDA

Greetings from STUART FLORIDA

Greetings from STUART FLORIDA

Greetings from STUART FLORIDA

Greetings from STUART FLORIDA

Greetings from STUART FLORIDA

Greetings from STUART FLORIDA

Greetings from STUART FLORIDA

Greetings from STUART FLORIDA

Greetings from STUART FLORIDA

Greetings from STUART FLORIDA

Greetings from STUART FLORIDA

Greetings from STUART FLORIDA

Greetings from STUART FLORIDA

Greetings from STUART FLORIDA

Greetings from STUART FLORIDA

Greetings from STUART FLORIDA

Printed in the USA
CPSIA information can be obtained
at www.ICGtesting.com
LVHW040533030624
781894LV00007B/797